6 STEPS TO EFFECTIVE WRITING IN CRIMINAL JUSTICE

6 STEPS TO EFFECTIVE WRITING IN CRIMINAL JUSTICE

Judy H. Schmidt, M. ED.
Harrisburg Area Community College

Michael K. Hooper, Ph.D.
California Department of Justice

WADSWORTH
CENGAGE Learning

Australia • Brazil • Japan • Korea • Mexico • Singapore • Spain • United Kingdom • United States

**6 Steps to Effective Writing
in Criminal Justice**
Judy H. Schmidt,
Michael K. Hooper

For product information and technology assistance, contact us at
Cengage Learning Customer & Sales Support, 1-800-354-9706.

For permission to use material from this text or product, submit all requests online at **www.cengage.com/permissions**.
Further permissions questions can be emailed to
permissionrequest@cengage.com.

ISBN-13: 978-0-534-17291-6
ISBN-10: 0-534-17291-1

Wadsworth
20 Davis Drive
Belmont, CA 94002-3098
USA

Cengage Learning is a leading provider of customized learning solutions with office locations around the globe, including Singapore, the United Kingdom, Australia, Mexico, Brazil, and Japan. Locate your local office at: **www.cengage.com/global**.

Cengage Learning products are represented in Canada by Nelson Education, Ltd.

To learn more about Wadsworth, visit
www.cengage.com/wadsworth.

Purchase any of our products at your local college store or at our preferred online store **www.ichapters.com**.

Printed in United States
12 13 14 15   12 11

TABLE OF CONTENTS

STEP ONE   1
THINKING ABOUT WRITING PROJECTS

STEP TWO   12
BUILDING THE PAPER'S STRUCTURE

STEP THREE   34
PREPARING TO WRITE

STEP FOUR   46
DRAFTING

STEP FIVE   60
REVISING AT THE CONTENT LEVEL

STEP SIX   74
REVISION: EVALUATING SENTENCE
STRUCTURE AND STYLE

APPENDIX A   86
PRACTITIONER RESEARCH REPORT
EXAMPLE

APPENDIX B   89
ADMINISTRATIVE REPORTS

APPENDIX C   92
INVESTIGATIVE REPORTS

PREFACE

Conceptually, effective writing is the ability to convey clearly thoughts on paper (or on a computer screen) for the benefit of an intended readership. *6 Steps to Effective Writing in Criminal Justice* develops a standard method for approaching writing tasks, whether academic or professional, that is both logical and efficient to produce writing that reflects purpose, audience, and scope. Writers are guided through a series of specific thinking and writing skills that writers can apply at each step of the writing process: thinking about writing, building structure, preparing to write, drafting, and revising.

Both authors have extensive teaching experience and have written for academic and professional criminal justice audiences. Professor Schmidt is an English instructor experienced in providing writing instruction to students and consultation to faculty and practitioners. Dr. Hooper is a practitioner who has prepared and reviewed the gamut of professional (and academic) reports and has taught both criminal justice college students and practitioners.
The authors have reviewed thousands of papers and reports and thus bring with them extraordinary in-depth knowledge of all facets of academic and professional writing. Their expertise enables them to recognize the common impediments to effective writing and at the same time to provide the corrective guidance that leads to clear written communications. In essence, the authors have isolated the fundamentals of good writing and presented them in a uniquely illustrative manner.

6 Steps to Effective Writing in Criminal Justice is *not* intended to be a grammar or usage text, as it barely addresses these topics which are readily available in myriad technical texts. Instead, this book's value is its service as a guide for *approaching* any writing assignment. The compact handbook's logical and conversational flow enables the user to page quickly through its succinct content and extract the pointers that are pertinent to the task at hand and quickly fashion a responsive document.

The authors wish to acknowledge the following two colleagues for their valuable contributions: Karen Finkenbinder, Police Education/Training Specialist, Pennsylvania Municipal Police

Officers' Education and Training Commission; and Kathy Brode, Writing Specialist at Pennsylvania State University at Harrisburg.

The authors also wish to acknowledge the following reviewers: Bruce Bikle, California State University-Sacramento; Roger Davis, California State University-Sacramento; Phyllis Gerstenfeld, California State University-Stanislaus; Mike Palmiotto, Wichita State University; and Jay Wachtel, CSU-Fullerton.

STEP ONE:
THINKING ABOUT WRITING
PROJECTS

GETTING STARTED

Imagine this. You are sitting in a classroom, hearing your instructor begin, "I would like you to write a paper...." She then goes on to mention specifics about the assignment requiring research and strong writing skills. Perhaps your first reaction is to feel somewhat overwhelmed and apprehensive, trying to decide how you will handle the assignment--and maybe certain that you can't do it!

In case you imagine you are the only person who reacts this way when asked to write, rest assured you have lots of company. In fact, many Criminal Justice majors and professionals in the field indicate they are uncomfortable knowing how to approach required academic and professional writing tasks. Because they are unaware of an efficient, effective manner for thinking and then writing, each assignment seems like a new test where no guidelines exist.

Taken to the extreme, some beginning writers may believe that good writing is genetic, and, if you're not born with it, you can't be a strong writer. They don't understand that good writing consists of learning specific skills and then applying them to the writing situation after they decipher the writing problem, not unlike learning to play golf, using a map to drive to a new location, or determining the murderer in a crime novel.

Therefore, the purpose of this compact resource manual is to help develop strong writing skills for you as Criminal Justice students that can be used now in academic classes and later in professional Criminal Justice writing. It develops a series of specific writing and thinking skills to be applied at each step of the writing process: thinking about writing, building structure, preparing to write, drafting, and revising. While many examples use Criminal Justice-specific topics, all writing skills can be readily applied to other courses and professional writing situations.

FOLLOWING THE PLANNING CLUES: TASK, SCOPE, AND READERS

Task

In our scenario above, when the beginning writer was feeling tense, a more confident, experienced writer was also listening with interest to the assignment. The major difference was that this student identified clues in the instructor's assignment, providing helpful information for the thinking about, planning for, and writing of the paper. The clues are: **task, scope, and readers**.

The **task** word(s) tells writers what writing action they will take with the information they have found which helps writers develop and reject ideas based on the assigned task.

Looking at the list of common **task** words following, note how each requires the reader to think about the information differently.

Task	Thinking Pattern
analyze	break into parts
compare	identify similarities
contrast	identify differences
critique	express opinion about specific aspects
define	give precise meaning; identify specific parts
develop	expand upon, elaborate
evaluate	appraise, judge
explain	give reasons for, make clear
identify	choose, select
illustrate	give examples of
interpret	explain the meaning or significance
review	reexamine, look over
summarize	condense; go over main points only

Notice that each task word directs the writer to different writing purposes and cannot be used interchangeably. If your instructor has written comments such as "unfocused," "didn't answer the question," or "confused purpose," chances are great that you did not meet the assignment's **task.**

SCOPE

After the writer has a basic understanding of the kind of thinking the paper will require, the **task**, it is important to consider another clue, the **scope,** which is the amount of material that would need to be covered to complete the writing tasks.

Consider these factors when determining **scope**:

- number and kinds of writing tasks in assignment
- required number of pages or words
- difficulties in finding research
- reader's knowledge of subject area

The first two factors, writing task and paper length, are easy to understand in terms of choosing a subject topic. But writers often miscalculate the scope, resulting in a subject topic that is too limited, leaving the writer with a lot of extra space to try to fill, or too broad, forcing the writer to cover material very superficially because there isn't time to cover it adequately. **Remember, not every subject topic fits every assignment.**

The third factor, difficulties in finding research, asks the writer to anticipate difficulties in finding the necessary research to develop the topic. Is the topic so broad that the writer would need months to gather necessary information? Is there very little research that could be done because the topic is too vague and undefined? Would the writer need some special permission to acquire research from sources? (Think government, military, personnel files, ongoing research here.) Is the topic so new that journal articles, or at least the ones most college/public libraries subscribe to, are not yet available?

Readers' knowledge of the subject is also a determining factor in choosing a subject topic. If identified readers know very little about the subject, the writer may have to "spend" a large number of pages to bring them to the "starting point" of the paper. Conversely, beginning writers may want to avoid a subject area when the readers are experts in the field, recognizing the writer's grasp of

4

information is still too elementary to capture reader interest. Writers should also assess subject topics for emotional reactions they may produce in readers. Of special concern are those subject topics that produce very opposite but equally strong feelings/beliefs in readers or positions that the writer already disagrees with.

READERS

The last writing clue to be considered at this thinking about stage is to identify who will read your paper. Generally, in academic classes, the reader is the instructor unless otherwise specified, while professional Criminal Justice correspondence may have levels of readers with reports often being circulated upward or used as court documents.

Whether academic or professional assignments, writers need to identify their **readers** to answer three important questions:

- What does the reader already know about this topic?
- What information does the reader need to know in order to understand this topic?
- What preconceptions, if any, does the reader have toward my topic?

ANALYZING A SAMPLE ASSIGNMENT

Only when writers look at a paper assignment in terms of the task to be accomplished, the scope of the assignment, and the readers can they begin to generate appropriate ideas.

Let's see how this would work. Suppose your Criminal Justice instructor gave your class this paper assignment.

The field of law enforcement provides a wide variety of research opportunities, interesting to both students and practitioners. Therefore, the purpose of this paper is first to ask you to identify a research topic that provides recent information to law enforcement practitioners that would be helpful to them in their crime prevention mission. To help you select a current topic, please review current CJ publications and/or interview law enforcement practitioners to gather possible ideas.

Then, after you have selected a writing topic, prepare a research paper that summarizes at least three key aspects of the current CJ area relating to crime prevention you have chosen that you judge practitioners would need to know in order to understand the information. The paper should be approximately ten pages, using at least five different research resources. All resources should be documented using APA documentation format. The due date is October 21, and the paper is worth 30 percent of the course grade.

As an added incentive to perform well on this exercise, a review panel of local police chiefs will read each paper to determine which three papers best address topics of urgent value to law enforcement.

Keeping this in mind, let's go back to the sample writing assignment to analyze it in terms of writing clues:

Task(s)	identify and summarize
Scope	approximately 10 pages
Reader	your instructor and local police chiefs

GENERATING IDEAS FOR WRITING TOPICS

Here's the good news: you have come up with a subject topic, so now you're ready to write the paper. Here's the bad news: no, you're not!

To believe that, after choosing a subject topic, the writer is now ready to write the paper is a mistake that many beginning writers make. This kind of thinking is like deciding to drive to a new location several states away and just getting in the car and driving or deciding that you want to build a log cabin home and starting to build without blueprints. You may eventually have limited success, but certainly the frustration level will be high as you use trial and error to accomplish your goal.

A better plan is to understand that thinking through your subject topic enables you to make important choices about a subject that interests you, to break it into smaller components, to determine research and resources you want to use and are available, and to develop an organizational plan to determine the order that information will be included in the text. Only then are you ready to begin drafting.

It's very difficult to write a strong paper about a weak idea. How often have you heard a classmate say, "I didn't know what to write about. If the instructor had given me a topic, I could have turned in a good paper"? Yet, at this level of education, one of the tests of your understanding of course material is to be able to apply it, in part by determining a specific writing focus that allows you to show your mastery of course information.

7

GENERATING IDEAS FOR SAMPLE ASSIGNMENT

Looking again at our sample writing assignment, let's list several possible subject topics we could write about in CJ areas that relate to crime prevention:

1 terrorism
2 gang-related crime
3 nutrition/exercise
4 racial profiling
5 technology

Because each listed subject is so broad, we need to come up with a method that allows us to break down the subject topics to more narrowed areas to see the smaller subject areas of each subject topic.

Several methods to explore the topic and narrow ideas for writing exist, including **brain drain, free writing, listing/outlining,** and **reading**. However, in order to any use of these techniques, the writer needs to consider **all** generated ideas before discarding any of them. Sometimes the best ideas are those that, at first glance, seem strange or unconnected to the assignment.

TECHNIQUES TO NARROW SUBJECT TOPICS

BRAIN DRAIN is a technique to discover what your brain may be thinking. First, write the subject topic on a sheet of paper; then take approximately 3-5 minutes to list everything you associate with the topic. Do not consciously think before writing or evaluate anything on the list until time is up. Then look at the list, put similar ideas together, but also consider those that have no connection to other items on the list. You may have identified a more narrowed topic.

FREE WRITING is similar to brain drain. Keeping the writing topic in mind, a writer writes for 5 minutes without stopping, recording everything that comes into mind, even ideas that are unrelated to the writing topic. If the writer is unable to think of anything, "I can't think of anything; nothing comes to mind," should be written until something pops into mind. The trick is to record all thoughts within the 5-minute period. When time is up, the writer reads what has been written, considers it, and circles any ideas that are more focused and of interest as a writing idea.

LISTING is a casual approach to discovering content with the writer recording ideas on a list to make frequent additions and deletions to it. The writer makes no attempt to evaluate the usefulness of what is listed or consider its relation to other listed items. This technique, often preferred by visual learners, allows the writer to keep track of what may be very separate ideas to consider or to discover that many ideas actually fit together to form a central idea. One of the advantages of an idea list is that it is easily tucked into a pocket, allowing the writer to look at it frequently, whether in line in the cafeteria, waiting for the movie to begin, or sitting at a desk.

OUTLINING requires the writer to have a more structured idea of the writing subject and the major pieces of information that would be necessary to develop it. Therefore, some outlines are produced after writers have used the other techniques listed here. The writer can use a formal outline format with Roman numerals, letters, and numbers or a topic outline form where the writer uses phrases to describe each section.

Who would opt outlining? Certainly no one who feels the urge to begin writing right away because outlining requires the writer first to have a clear idea of writing direction. Writers in technical fields seem to choose this method that can create a "blueprint" writing plan, that is, everything decided and structured before drafting begins.

Don't let this scare you away from using it. The outline format provides a visual record that helps writers spot areas that are missing or weak, directing the writer to think through content and spot flaws in organization.

READING about the topic helps writers break down the subject topic into smaller parts because the reader often finds articles that deal with narrowed topics. And, if the narrowed topics are still large or complex, the writer may determine the subject topic may not be appropriate for the assignment task, scope, or readers. Reading has an additional function: it may show the writer how little he/she knows about the topic or challenge existing opinions/beliefs.

When a paper assignment is given, resist the impulse to begin writing the paper immediately. Instead, spend time analyzing and understanding the assignment, considering **task**, **scope**, and **readers** to help the writer identify possible writing topics.

Using this process is a good start in planning, but writing topics then need to be narrowed to develop a writing idea. **Brain drain, free writing, listing and outlining,** and **reading** are methods to help writers break the writing topic into smaller pieces of information to discover the writing idea for the assigned paper. In Chapter Two our listed subject topics are narrowed, using techniques discussed in this chapter.

It's natural for us to want to plunge into the writing project, immediately producing written pages, rather than spending time thinking and planning. However, by spending time understanding the writing project and giving ourselves time to generate and test ideas, we will save time later in the writing process, without trying to unravel writing snarls.

STEP TWO:
BUILDING THE PAPER'S
STRUCTURE

It would be so easy if only your instructor chose to tell you what to write about, which could eliminate so much thinking, much the same way you knew in grade school that you would begin each year's English class with the perennially exciting composition, "How I Spent my Summer Vacation."

Yet, since the purpose of college is to grow intellectually and to learn how to think critically to discover connections among information, writers first make a series of decisions about a paper's direction that builds the structure of the paper. Later it will be filled in with pertinent information and organized to meet readers' needs.

Three of the structural decisions this chapter looks at are: **narrowing the writing topic, gathering information from library sources, interviews and surveys, and then determining a tentative thesis statement.** (The tentative thesis statement will be mentioned in this chapter, but refer to Chapter 3 for a more complete discussion.)

Narrowing the Subject Topic

In Chapter 1 we discussed techniques that allow the writer to both generate and then narrow subject topics into smaller chunks of information, all focused on crime prevention. The problem is that the subject topics we generated in Chapter 1 are too broad and could not be handled in 10 pages, the scope of this writing assignment. Because we would have to skim over points too briefly to develop information, sort of a "drive-by" approach, fast and too busy to stop, we still need to narrow the subject topic to something we can develop intelligently, correlating to **task, scope, readers.**

Looking at the narrowed subjects below, you can see that we are beginning to move in more specific and focused directions. This in turn will give us a better idea of the research we will want to find.

Subject Topic	Narrowed Subject
Terrorism	airport security measures, computer-generated investigation, intelligence flow, threat assessment
Gang Crime	violence, drug use and marketing, intelligence gathering, anti-gang strategies, urban gangs, rural gangs

Nutrition/Exercise	Stress reduction, mandatory exercise programs, police officer dietary practices, enhanced performance, absenteeism reduction
Racial Profiling	definition, prevalence, anti-racial profiling training programs, patterns, negative impact, historical perspective, constitutional issues
Technology	computer-aided dispatch, crime mapping, crime analysis, computer crime, depersonalization, electronic monitoring

Note: Even though we have narrowed the topic from very general to more specific, we still need to evaluate the narrowed topic in terms of the assignment. Because we are not being asked only to gather information **about** a topic, we must consider, "What about this narrowed topic connects to the idea of practitioners and crime prevention?"

14

Gathering Information

Because we are **not** experts in the field, we don't know the answers and instead need to gather relevant information in order to decide if we're going in the right direction. The way to begin the process is by **researching relevant information from library sources, interviews, and surveys of appropriate subject matter experts.**

The **researched information** we find has three purposes:

1. it helps the writer continue to narrow and refine the subject topic
2. it helps the reader to determine how information fits together (the thesis statement)
3. it provides specific information to support and illustrate the paper's thesis statement

RESEARCH

It's easy to feel intimidated in the library, wondering where to look and what to look for. At this point, because we are exploring more general subject topics, we want to look at more general references from books, databases, periodicals, and on-line sources. Who is the best person to talk to about what to look at? The **reference librarian**, who probably has more suggestions about where to start than you have questions. Did you take the library tour during orientation? If not, the reference librarian can show you where information is located and even how to use the computerized library systems.

While you may be using more general reference resources, you should also be aware of special Criminal Justice resources. (Yes, the reference librarian knows about them, too.)

Some of the possible sources for reading in Criminal Justice to be considered could be some of the popular trade publications in the field, e.g., *Police Chief, Crime Control Digest,* or *FBI Law Enforcement Bulletin.* There are also numerous Criminal Justice academic journals, e.g., *Criminology* and *Policing,* documenting the results of research on current issues of research to both practitioners and academicians. In addition, there are numerous books on contemporary issues in Criminal Justice.

In recent years the federal government has subsidized numerous entities, e.g., National Institute of Justice and National Criminal Justice Reference Service, which have as their principal mission research to further Criminal Justice problem solving.

These research enterprises publish their findings in a wide array of publications, many of which are available through their web sites or through colleges' and universities' collections. The research findings are both contemporary and easily understood; they're written principally for practitioners, who generally prefer summarized, straightforward information. Therefore, both beginning and more advanced students are able to access and understand these resources.

Of course, as sources for reading go, there is always the "wonderful world of the Web." Currently, many Criminal Justice agencies have their own web sites, and a review of them can give insights into subject areas being researched. However, writers must be careful when accessing information from Internet sources; some are credible while others are not. Please refer to Chapter 3, "Evaluating Sources," where we provide suggestions for determining the credibility of a source. Additionally, your instructor and librarians can provide assistance in source evaluation.

READING RESEARCH

Beginning writers often are not selective about choosing which resources to take out of the library. They tend to copy faithfully everything they have read without considering its relationship to the topic and other gathered information. And somehow, they equate the paper volume of information with having gathered enough information to begin to write.

While it's gratifying to find the research material we were looking for, the writer has to understand what each source means. The content certainly communicates information, but it also gives the writer a clear picture of whether the topic is still too broad, would require the writer to have previous understanding of the topic, or would require the writer to give extensive background to the readers.

Furthermore, without understanding the content, writers have no idea whether it relates to our ever-narrowing topic, nor do they understand its relationship to other sources. Do they agree, contradict each other, or duplicate the same idea?

READING TIPS

- Survey the source before reading. Look at the table of contents, any information listed about the author, and, if applicable, the summary or abstract directly under the title that will tell you what the article is about.
- Note the author's credentials and look at the publisher of the material.***

- Read the material quickly the first time to get a general idea of content and format. Do not highlight or underline.
- Read the material again, this time slowly; underline or highlight <u>sparingly</u>. Often writers mark too much so nothing really stands out.
- Annotate (make notes about content) in the margins so you can later find the information in the material.
- Write a summary of the article content, 2-3 sentences either at the top of your copy or in a small research notebook, and give the thesis statement
- Collect all bibliographic material you will need to reference the source in your paper.
- Identify the source as a primary source (the document itself) or a secondary source (something written about the document itself). Think here of the difference between using the "Declaration of Independence" (primary) vs. a history book that discusses the importance of the document (secondary source).

**This information will be valuable later when we discuss evaluating resources in Chapter 3.

Interviews

Although a review of the written materials on a topic is usually the best place to begin research, an interview can be an important addition to the information-seeking process. An interview is a structured conversation. It can be most useful for obtaining information and/or direction to the most current information on a topic after initial reading has been done.

An interview also may be valuable for developing examples to support ideas gained from reading. Too, interviewing an expert in a specific subject may allow the writer to gain clarification on concepts that may not be readily understood when reading research, e.g., "specific intent" versus "general intent" crimes or "racial profiling."

Obviously, the value of an interview largely depends on who is being interviewed. Not everyone connected with a subject will be the right person to provide the best information on the topic, so writers first need to be careful that selected interviewees are knowledgeable in the field. Therefore, writers might first want to consider interviewing instructors and practitioners.

Within academic institutions, instructors can often guide students to other faculty members who might be helpful sources of information, or a directory that lists faculty members by their teaching and research interests may exist. Academicians generally adhere to the scientific method in their own research endeavors so that their comments are usually based on what the findings of quality research have revealed. Therefore, we might consider their findings to be fairly objective.

In contrast, when selecting an interviewee from the practitioner realm, or from the community, the interviewer should be aware of possible subjectivity. For example, if a writer were preparing a research paper on "three strikes legislation," opinions and knowledge bases could be biased, depending on the interviewee's position within the criminal justice system. For example, a representative from the jail or prison system could be concerned about overcrowding while the local police chief may be motivated by taking criminals out of circulation to the maximum extent possible. Therefore, when interviewing practitioners, it is important to be sensitive to position bias. Also, practitioners are not always familiar with the state of scientific research on a subject. Of course, practitioners do have a very good experience-based sense of the realities affecting a situation or how scientific findings actually apply in the "real world."

CONDUCTING INTERVIEWS

As an interviewer, a writer should conform to some time-tested principles of interviewing. First, the writer should not presume that the person identified for a possible interview is indeed the best source for information. Therefore, when the potential interviewee is contacted, the interviewer should be precise and clear about the topic of the interview and the information to be elicited. If the person confirms knowledge of the subject matter, the interviewer should set up an interview date and time, ensuring at least 30 minutes for the interview. If the person claims not to be knowledgeable on the subject of the interview or for any other reason cannot be interviewed, an effective interview technique is to ask if the person can recommend someone else to speak with.

Once an appointment has been arranged, the next step is for the interviewer to prepare questions for the interview. A well-prepared interviewer can gain the respect of the interviewee and inspire quality responsiveness. Questions should be open-ended and fair. Open-ended questions are those that cannot be answered with a simple "yes" or "no." A question such as "Do you believe in the death penalty?" should be recast as, "What is your opinion of the death penalty?" The second question elicits a thoughtful, detailed response as compared to the first one that calls for only a one-word answer. As regards "fairness," asking awkward or inflammatory questions often begets a similar response.

An example of this occurred recently when a well-known television personality interviewed a congressman suspected of involvement in the disappearance of a Washington, D.C., intern. Shortly after the nationally televised interview got underway, the interviewer asked bluntly of the congressman, "Did you kill Chandra Levy?" Whatever the intended result of the question, one thing it did not do was foster responsiveness.

Another potential interviewing pitfall is using leading questions, e.g., "Why do so many college students drink excessively?" or "Why are members of minorities disproportionately involved in drug use?" Note that each question assumes certain things, i.e., student alcohol abuse and drug involvement, which the interviewee may not agree with. Keep in mind that the interviewer's purpose is to find out what the interviewee knows, not misuse the occasion to express the interviewer's personal opinion or to influence the direction of the response.

INTERVIEW TIPS

While there are no lists of questions that all interviewers should use, here are a few general suggestions:

1. Review the questions you intend to ask before the interview to ensure they are clear or not too long or complicated.
2. Make sure that multiple questions are not embedded in a single one.
3. Make certain that questions are designed to gather biographical and background information about the interviewee to establish credibility and validity of remarks.

Before the interview begins, the interviewer needs to ask permission to videotape or audiotape the interview. If taping is approved, it is still a good idea to take notes on key points in case of mechanical failure and also later to help locate segments of the taping. Because an interview is a structured conversation, the interviewer should feel comfortable asking questions to help clarify information that seems confusing or incomplete. Otherwise, the interviewer who later becomes the writer will find it difficult to report on information that was not completely understood.

Asking follow-up questions is another important interviewing technique for gathering information. Often an interviewee may introduce an idea relating to the research subject that the interviewer may not have anticipated but now understands as an important trend of thought or to clarify what may seem to be contradictory information.

Practiced interviewers, after completing their listed questions, will ask, "Is there anything else that you think I should know?" This is done in the event the interviewee had assumed the interviewer already had knowledge of key elements of a subject because questions were not asked about them. Additionally, it gives the interviewee the opportunity to share information that may not be the focus of the interview but that may be closely related and helpful in providing perspective on the research subject or tentative thesis.

Obviously, the good interviewer will remember manners and thank the interviewee for the opportunity to speak, also requesting the opportunity to contact again should any clarification be necessary. Later, sending a copy of the final paper is a recommended practice that can be gratifying for the interviewee and also maintain positive relations for any subsequent interviewing or surveying that may be required (Williams & Brydon-Miller, 1997, pp.50-52).

USING INTERVIEWS TO DISCOVER DIRECTION

We said earlier that interviewing is a strategy for discovering direction, either by showing the writer a variety of ideas about a subject area or introducing conflicting ideas about the subject, alerting the writer that possibilities for further research exist.

As you read the following fictitious interviews conducted by Andrew, our guest writer, note that the **narrowed ideas** from the beginning of this chapter are mentioned in the course of the interviews. However, note that Andrew unexpectedly discovers that most interviewees want to talk about community policing, but they all have different opinions about its importance and its application to crime prevention.

In "real life," this twist of ideas that swirls together what the interviewer thought he was going to talk about and an unanticipated direction--community policing—developed by the interviewees may lead the writer into a new and workable paper topic.

Read through the following interviews, trying to project how you think Andrew will piece together interview information and what will be his tentative thesis.

ROBERTA DOMINGO, CHIEF OF POLICE,
MILLVIEW POLICE DEPARTMENT
TUESDAY, MAY 14

Chief Domingo indicated she was very interested in what
the research has shown to be the recipe for effective
community policing. She related that when she was
appointed to her present position, the Mayor of Millview
took her aside and told her that he expected two principal
accomplishments within two years: a nationally accredited
police department and implementation of community
policing.

The Chief said she has started to convert her agency to a
community policing style of policing but isn't certain she's
implementing it in its textbook form, which the National
Accrediting Agency would expect. The Chief said she'd be
most interested in seeing some relatively brief document
that covered the "essentials of community policing—kind of
a cookbook on how to best set it up."

ROBERT DEMPSEY, SHERIFF, GRANITE COUNTY
SHERIFF'S DEPARTMENT
WEDNESDAY, MAY 15

I began my interview with Sheriff Dempsey by saying that I
had already spoken with Chief Domingo. Sheriff Dempsey
quickly related that he thought highly of Chief Domingo
but added, "Her territory is entirely different from mine."
The Sheriff explained that the Chief's jurisdiction was
largely urban and also a bit "up-scale." He further
explained, "The geographic region for which I'm
responsible is mostly rural and the neighbors rarely see
each other. As far as crime is concerned, they're mainly

concerned about the drunk drivers that seem to be increasing in number as the city encroaches on the farmland.

PETULA HARRISON, COMMUNITY RELATIONS OFFICER, CLEARSTREAM POLICE DEPARTMENT THURSDAY, MAY 16

Officer Harrison said that a lot of people within her department really fail to recognize the value of community policing. Many of the officers think it translates to setting up community service programs or holding so-called "crime-stopper" programs for the public to attend. They fail to understand that community policing with its problem-solving component extends to all aspects of policing.

Because Officer Harrison seemed to possess abundant knowledge on community policing, I asked her what might be a best source for local and national statistics on the subject. She said that I need go no further than the book shelf in her office for local reports and statistics on the subject. She said I was welcome to peruse her collection of local agencies' programs. As regards the big picture, she referred me back to my college library and said to check out a publication called *Sourcebook of Criminal Justice Statistics*, published by the Bureau of Justice Statistics. She told me that this federally financed publication contained some good information on the national community policing picture.

As I was about to conclude the interview, Officer Harrison said that she did want to ensure that I got a full range of views on community policing. She suggested I speak with veteran officer, John Knowitall, who she said was openly anti-community policing.

25

JOHN KNOWITALL, PATROL OFFICER, CLEARSTREAM POLICE DEPARTMENT
THURSDAY, MAY 16

I gave Officer Knowitall background on my assignment.
He said, "I'll tell you what would be highly beneficial to
controlling crime in Clearstream: reduction in paperwork!"
He said that he spends much more time on completing
reports than he does on patrol—or even outside the station
house. "If I could get free of the paperwork burden, I'd be
able to spend much more time in the field doing real police
work—putting bad guys in jail!" He also commented
negatively about the new policing strategy that his chief
was attempting to impose upon the patrol force:
community policing. His view was that it would never
work: "It was some liberal's idea of taking a soft approach
toward criminals."

REBECCA FARMER, DEPUTY, GRANITE COUNTY SHERIFF'S DEPARTMENT
FRIDAY, MAY 17

Deputy Rebecca Farmer had been inside the sheriff's station
when I met with Sheriff Dempsey. She had that, after I'd
finished interviewing him to look her up. She was curious
about the Sheriff's view as important for preventing crime.
I indicated how concerned he seemed to be about the drunk
driving problem. The deputy responded, "Oh yes, that's
his big concern. The local MADD chapter has been on him
constantly of late to take some enforcement action." They've
asked him to look into the community policing strategy and
see if that might work for our county. His reply has always
been, " 'That stuff won't work for problems like drunk
driving. "

BARNARD FIFE, DEPUTY, GRANITE COUNTY
SHERIFF'S DEPARTMENT
FRIDAY, MAY 17

Deputy Fife was the deputy in charge of the jail when I
interviewed Deputy Farmer. He'd overheard the interview
and motioned me over after Deputy Farmer had completed
her interview and returned to her patrol duties. Deputy
Fife said, "Do you know what's really needed around
here?" He then volunteered, "We need the 'brass' to take
some computer training! If they could gain a greater
understanding of what technology offers, then we'd be
much further along in preventing crime. There are some
incredible programs out there that can almost predict where
and when crimes will occur. I've read in *Law Enforcement
Technology* that lots of police and sheriff departments are
depending on something called crime analysis to map
crimes and deploy their patrol units."

LAWRENCE LIPTON, PATROL OFFICER,
MILLVIEW POLICE DEPARTMENT
SATURDAY, MAY 18

I was referred to Officer Lipton by Chief Domingo. Lipton
had a reputation as an expert on effective policing
strategies. He had recently been placed in charge of the
police department's crime analysis unit. Officer Lipton was
very pleased to spend time with me after hearing that I was
offering my research services. In fact, he said, "Do I have
just the project for you!" He related that while he had
sound computer skills and was able to generate crime
maps, he had scant resources to deploy in the detected
crime "hot spots." He said that he'd heard that the concept
of community policing somehow used citizens to directly
assist in crime fighting. He was far too familiar with his
department's weak capabilities to be proactive—rather than

27

reactive—as a result of simply too few cops and hoped for a strategy to be implemented that would effectively expand the patrol force's "eyes and ears." He added that, as far as he knew, no one on the police department really understood community policing and how it really was supposed to operate.

LESLIE TEA, PATROL OFFICER, MILLVIEW POLICE DEPARTMENT
SATURDAY, MAY 18

Officer Tea was an officer who had been assigned to work with Officer Lipton in setting up the ideal community policing framework. She had no special expertise in the subject of community policing but had been assigned to assist Lipton because of her rapport with the African-American community. The African-American community had in recent years called attention to a succession of perceived injustices. Tea had exhibited commendable leadership in successfully calming the outcry, which she thought was attributable to her ability to work with gang leaders. She had heard how community policing had worked in some major urban areas to defuse the gang problem. She'd be interested in seeing any research that pointed to effective methods for impacting the gang problem.

PAT OCEAN, DEPUTY, GRANITE COUNTY SHERIFF'S DEPARTMENT
MONDAY, MAY 20

I visited the sheriff's department one additional time to get a "gut" reaction from the first deputy I encountered. That

28

person was Deputy Pat Ocean. Deputy Ocean wasted no time in responding to how I might be of research assistance. He immediately responded, "Read as much as you can on terrorism, kid. We ain't seen nuthin' yet!" When I asked him what would be a good proactive path to pursue to combat terrorism, he answered my question with a question: "Have you ever tried to contend with a termite infestation?" He then added, "Ya know, we're just gonna have to go into every place where the terrorists reside and 'tent' the area and then fumigate." I didn't altogether understand the officer's prescription, but I did form an opinion that it might not be productive to pursue the interview.

ANDREW'S ANALYSIS

As Andrew read through his interview notes, he realized the majority of interviews revealed "community policing" as a central focus. It was mentioned specifically in five interviews, three in a positive vein and two with negative overtones. Additionally, three other interviews addressed crime issues that Andrew's research reading had already shown were functions of community policing: use of other agencies to address criminal matters, "crime analysis," and use of the community's "eyes and ears."

Yet, Andrew noted those interviewed had different definitions of what community policing entails, alerting him it might be a good idea to pursue, especially in terms of the paper **task** and **readers.** Therefore, researching articles about community policing and looking at what the interviewees had to say should help Andrew to discover the point he will support, the **thesis statement,** which we begin to discuss a bit later in this chapter.

SURVEYS

Surveying is another method for learning more about a topic, supporting a thesis, or discovering direction. Surveying generally connotes a wide and objective search for information or opinions. A survey is often administered in a less personal fashion than an interview although surveys could be given during an interview. Very often surveys are conducted through the mail or via telephone. They also can be administered via e-mail or by other electronic means, e.g., via the Web. Surveys are popular with many researchers because a large number of individuals can be reached at a minimal expense.

In general, survey questions have to be clear and to the point. As has already been mentioned in the context of interviewing, survey questions should not be biased or leading. The survey questionnaires should not take longer than 15 minutes to complete. Making the survey form attractive to the eye will have a positive impact on the response rate.

It is important to recognize that information gathered via surveying is only as useful as the manner in which it was collected. It is essential that bias be controlled to the maximum extent possible. This is accomplished through use of sound research design principles, covered in depth in basic research methods courses. However, while this writing supplement for Criminal Justice students is not intended to be a primer for research methods, there is one critically important aspect of methods courses that has bearing here: random sampling.

Randomness in surveying means that everyone in a given population has an equal chance of being selected for questioning. Use of a survey usually implies that at least 30 people will be questioned, a number selected for statistical purposes.

Thus, if we want to gain insights into critical issues of concern to policing executives, the surveying is limited to the geographic boundaries of the region sampled. However, the value in this is that so long as all persons in a given area have an equal chance of being included in the survey, a random sampling method is used to select the survey participants, guaranteeing the findings can apply to that entire population.

As a case in point, the authors of this manual recently conducted a mail survey (with fax as a response option) of police executives from California and Pennsylvania. The questionnaire elicited "top research priorities." Questionnaire recipients were selected, randomly, from comprehensive rosters of both states' chief executives. Every third chief listed on the rosters was sent a survey form. By using this random method, we would be able to stand on solid ground if anyone were to question the survey results in terms of their representing both states' chiefs' overall perspectives. Interestingly, among the top four categories of research interest was an area categorized as "written communications/report writing." The underlying research question was "What can be done to improve the quality of officers' written communications?" (Perhaps supplying them with a copy of this manual?) For the record, the other three categories of research interest were community oriented policing, technology, and ethics.

Surveying should be viewed as an extensive undertaking that often does not involve one-on-one exchanges with the respondent. Its value lies in the large numbers of persons it can poll. The decision to interview versus survey, or to do both, or neither, is dependent on the information gap and the available time/resources for completion.

The sample assignment used in this text for illustrative purposes is the type that could involve interviewing or surveying although the timeline for report completion might be too short for a survey or survey and interviews. Because of the brevity if this text, we have not provided exemplar survey questionnaires.

The Tentative Thesis Statement

In Chapter 3 we'll discuss the **tentative thesis statement**, our third structural element, which is the result of thinking and gathering information. This tentative thesis statement then directs future thinking about which informational sources to use, how they fit together, and which organizational plan will be used to develop the paper content.

Take a look at the flowchart on the next page to understand how everything discussed up to this point works together to help us build the paper's structure and guide later decisions.

Writing Assignment

Generate Ideas

Task   Scope   Readers

Identify Appropriate Ideas

Interview   Research   Survey

Analyze

Tentative Thesis

(Cooley, 1993, p. 13)

At this point we label it **tentative thesis** because writers will continue to modify the thesis as they continue to gather and assess additional information.

References

Cooley, M.E. (1993). *The inventive writer: Using critical Thinking to persuade.* Lexington, MA: D.C. Heath.

Williams, B.T., & Brydon-Miller, M. (1997). *Concept to Completion: Writing well in the social sciences.* New York: Harcourt Brace College Publishers.

STEP THREE:
PREPARING TO WRITE

In the previous chapter, we looked at **narrowing the writing topic** and **gathering information through library research and interviews/surveys**. At that point in the paper writing process, we were concerned with finding information relating to the topic rather than selecting information that supported a position the paper will develop.

Even if we began to research with an idea of what we hoped to support, such as the negative effects of daycare on six year olds, many of our sources may have focused on information about "daycare" or "six year olds." Therefore, the writer's challenge is to look at how research sources meet, that is, how they fit together to develop and support a specific position. The sentence in the paper that tells our readers the idea we plan to develop and support is called the **thesis statement**. Let's take time to define exactly what we mean by this term.

DETERMINING A TENTATIVE THESIS

The final piece of structure, **determining a tentative thesis**, can happen only after a writer narrows the topic and conducts some research to gather specific information. The **thesis** then is the writer's <u>reasoned</u> conclusion about how information fits together or the position that will be supported by research. This doesn't mean that there is one conclusion or correct meaning only. Instead, the writer's goal is to prove to the reader that the writer's thesis is reasonable or valid, based on information, not opinion or emotion. This reasoned conclusion is contained in a sentence called the **thesis statement.**

Some beginning writers misunderstand the sequential process of **thinking about** and **narrowing the topic,** **finding research resources,** and then **determining a thesis statement.** Instead, these inexperienced writers first develop a thesis idea, reflecting their own opinions, and then go to the library to try to find information to support the thesis idea.

This misunderstanding of process creates major problems. First, it leads to generalizations and somewhat unsophisticated thinking, reflecting bias instead of knowledge. For example, a pre-determined thesis statement might be, "Daycare is <u>bad</u> for <u>all children</u> under <u>six years old</u>."

Not only has the writer carved out huge areas to write about- all daycare and all six year olds, but, even more importantly, has substituted an illogical generalization for a specific thesis statement. Why was this done? Because the writer thought it would be faster to make the research support the thesis rather than look at research to arrive at a thesis statement. This approach of forming thesis statement first and then researching most often results in faulty generalizations that can't be supported.

The second problem with determining the thesis and then looking for information that supports it is just that: the writer ignores research that doesn't support the thesis, the sort of "I'm not looking" approach that often results in invalid conclusions. Using our example, research exists to show preschool children in daycare may be more independent, may learn how to relate collaboratively, may become more self-sufficient than children at home, information the writer would have to ignore. **Therefore, our thesis statement needs to reflect accurately what reliable research resources will support**.

It's really not difficult to arrive at a **thesis statement,** but there are mistakes to avoid. Consider the list below of common errors writers make when writing the thesis statement.

1. The thesis statement announces the topic rather than states a position. "This paper is about new security measures in airports."
2. The thesis is too vague or broad to convey meaning to readers or to give specific support. "The average college student today is much more advanced than students twenty years ago."
3. The thesis is too specific or narrow to write about. "Seventy-two percent of freshmen on this campus brought their own computers to college."

Now that we know what the thesis statement is <u>not</u>, we need to consider how to "get" one.

SYNTHESIZING SOURCES TO ARRIVE AT A THESIS STATEMENT

If you recall, we started out our paper-writing process by analyzing task, scope, readers, then narrowed to a writing topic through some preliminary researching/interviewing/surveying. We may even have had some idea of what we thought we might find in our research, but that was based more on opinion rather than resources.

Yet, as we collect information about the writing topic, what we read changes our thinking. Our research process begins to shape us as we find a variety of informational sources that broaden our knowledge of the topic, identify current, often contradictory, issues within the topic that make us realize our initial **tentative thesis statement** is no longer valid or quite on the mark.

Using our thesis example of daycare and six year olds, we noted that the writer had used opinion to develop the thesis statement, "Daycare is harmful to all six year olds." But through careful gathering of sources the writer may have discovered the following:

1. The term "daycare" can be applied to a variety of different childcare situations, differing in purpose, number of hours spent, identity of caregivers, etc.
2. The original term "harmful" could refer to a number of different elements including developmental, psychological, or physical factors.
3. There may be trade-offs between the benefits and negative effects of daycare for a particular age that may make a blanket statement about harm less valid.

Therefore, by gathering information and comparing/contrasting the information in our resources, we have the chance to rethink/reevaluate our tentative thesis statement. We call this putting together of resources **"synthesis"** or **"synthesizing" our sources.**

THE SYNTHESIS MAP

It's hard to find a method that allows a writer to look at all the sources together to take an inventory of the information that has been gathered. This process, called **synthesizing,** allows the reader to see how sources "fit" together i.e., duplicate, contradict, build upon others, to determine

which sources to hold on to and which no longer fit or are
necessary.

There is, of course, the possibility of spreading out the
source material on a large surface such as your living room
floor or the dorm hallway…. But even spreading all
material out would still leave the task of crawling around
from source to source, looking at each source individually
and collectively to understand the content.

An alternate method for **synthesizing** sources easily is to
create a chart that allows us to look at what each source
develops individually and compare/contrast with other
sources. (**Note:** If the writer has followed the reading
research suggestions in Chapter 1, much of the work for
filling in the chart has already been done.)

EXAMPLE OF SYNTHESIS MAP

Source Title *Problem Oriented Policing*	Source Title *Fixing Broken Windows*	Source Title *Community Policing: How to Get Started*	Source Title *Law Enforcement News*
Thesis Statement of source Crime control requires getting at the root of the problem	**Thesis Statement of source** A strong relationship exists between blight and crime	**Thesis Statement of source** Police-community partnership is the essence of community policing	**Thesis Statement of source** Combating terrorism requires community involvement.
Major Points	**Major Points**	**Major Points**	**Major Points**
1. S.A.R.A. methodology for problem solving	1. Conditions of disrepair signal no street guardianship ("Broken Windows")	1. COP is a philosophy for total police agency	1. Linking police and the citizens for information gathering

2. Proactivity-getting at the underlying dynamics of a crime problem	2. Community mobilization required to address disrepair	2. Essence of COP is police-public partnership, with "trust" as the "glue"	2.
3.	3. Government agencies beyond the police must be involved	3. Underlying theory: normative sponsorship and critical social theory	3.

SYNTHESIS MAP FUNCTION

In a sense, this chart provides a snapshot of all gathered information. The writer can then trace connections from source to source, making sure that similar ideas in fact are contained in each source. In chart form the writer has a map of everything "owned" and can make decisions about which sources to keep and which sources to discard because they no longer reflect the developing idea. The writer can then identify information gaps in remaining sources and begin searching for additional research.

But here is a surprising result of using the **synthesis map**: writers often find connections that they hadn't thought about before or realized existed. This discovery may lead writers to pursue an entirely different direction for the paper, scrapping one tentative thesis idea for another.

This reassessment of information and its connection to other information, leading to new understandings/conclusions, mimics how we think. We always add additional information or reassess what we know to draw different conclusions. How often do we and others say that we made the best decisions based on what we knew at the time,

39

meaning that with later information we might have drawn different conclusions.

Perhaps a sad analogy to this point is the post "9-11" reappraisal of information. Surveillance reports and FBI requests, INS spotty monitoring of those in the United States with student visas, and the identification of a pattern of flight school enrollment had little individual significance, but, later examined together, the pieces had a distressing connection.

In short, the **synthesis map** allows the writer to make writing/thinking decisions about the future direction of the paper by performing the following tasks:
1. **evaluate** validity of sources and eliminate some sources
2. **identify** and resolve gaps/conflicts in information
3. **readjust** the tentative thesis to become the prime time thesis
4. **discover** a different or modified thesis statement

Evaluating Validity of Sources

Most writers know that at some point they will have to sort through the stacks of photocopied sheets of research to identify "treasures" and put the rest in the discard pile. One of the first issues to consider when synthesizing sources is to consider the **validity** of the source.

Many writers might assume that **validity** only means that the information is reliable. Certainly that's important and increasingly more complicated with Internet research capabilities and advertising/promotional materials closely mimicking educational/scientific formats. Therefore, writers must examine each source of gathered material rather than assuming that it is valid because it is in print.

How does the writer evaluate the validity? Let's consider questions writers should ask themselves when looking at sources to determine **validity.**

DETERMINING VALIDITY

1. What do I know about this source? Does the library subscribe to it? Is it from a reputable Internet source?
2. How current is the information given in the source? If it is less current, the possibility is greater that information has been changed/amplified since the original publication date. Therefore, it may no longer be valid in light of further research/information.
3. Is the authority cited in the source an authority in the field being discussed? Are the authority's credentials/degrees reputable?
4. Does the reputable source carry a predictable bias, that is, maintain a consistent, predictable point-of-view because of the writer/publication's position? Think here about sources that have either a liberal or conservative political view, or a health magazine that predictably will promote the value of good diet and exercise. While this predictable bias doesn't mean the information isn't factual, we can expect that it will not carry an opposing point of view.
5. Am I getting conflicting information from sources? If this happens, conventional wisdom suggests going with the majority unless the dissenting voice is considered to be the major authority in the field.

Identifying and Resolving Gaps in Information

Because we have been so wise to consider information gaps now rather than discovering them in the midst of writing the paper (the day before it's due), we have the opportunity to eliminate and/or gather additional information needed to develop and support either the thesis statement developed previously or the new thesis statement that popped out when we synthesized our sources.

If we could list one of the major mistakes writers make at this point, it would be the writer who tries to "make do" with sources, attempting to stretch them to appear to support/develop ideas, when the reader realizes little support exists. Such writers either evaluate readers as less perceptive or lack the initiative/energy to go retrieve more information. Now, of course, if you're trying to write a paper for the next day's class....

Information gaps or need for additional information don't indicate we were bad researchers. Instead, as noted before, we may have significantly changed our intended focus (thesis statement) as a result of information gathered or discovered that we could not find the resource material we thought we could find. The latter is especially true when we are researching for very recent information. There may be a significant publishing gap between events/discoveries and the publication of that information as Andrew, our guest writer, has discovered.

The interviews conducted in the course of researching his sample paper convinced Andrew that some police forces needed a greater understanding of the core features of community policing.

The interviews also revealed an interest in a policing strategy that would create a "one- size-fits-all" approach to the problems confronting police. Some of the problems interviewees cited were drunk driving, gangs, and terrorism. Therefore, Andrew concluded he needed to find more information that showed how community policing might be used successfully to counter such community problems.

Going to the library, Andrew easily found on-line research reports supporting the value of community policing in attacking the gang problem, including The National Institute of Justice web site (www.ojp.usdoj.gov/nij), a Department of Justice research agency and sponsor of the National Criminal Justice Reference Service (NCJRS), that had subsidized a large number of research studies on this topic. From reading, Andrew discovered an Office of Juvenile Justice and Delinquency Prevention (OJJDP) had been created within the Department of Justice specifically to research gangs and juvenile violence. This research conducted by OJJDP was readily accessible via the web site of the National Criminal Justice Reference Center Service, www.ncjrs.org. In fact, while looking at OJJDP materials he also found a study, "A Guide to Combating Juvenile DUI," that also covered the topic of DUI.

So far so good, but locating materials on how community policing could impact terrorism was a bit of a challenge because many events have been too recent for scholarly publications, addressing the issue, to appear. Andrew's accessing conventional sites on the web did not turn up examples of community policing addressing terrorism, so he decided to use another resource, i.e., paying a visit to one of the well-informed campus professors, Professor Radcliffe.

As Andrew had hoped, Professor Radcliffe had wasted no time in gathering materials on the subject of "homeland" terrorism because it had become an important topic of discussion in Radcliffe's "Contemporary Issues" course. He showed Andrew the latest edition of *Community Links*, which featured an article entitled "The Community Becomes First Line of Defense." He also provided guidance to a recent article on terrorism, "Secret Weapon Against Terrorism? Chiefs Say Community Policing is an Ace in the Hole," that appeared in the John Jay College of Criminal Justice publication, *Law Enforcement News*.

ADJUSTING THE THESIS STATEMENT

Remember that we said the tentative thesis was a starting point, reflecting what we intended to support, based on preliminary research? Therefore, the tentative thesis continues to be modified, based on what we discover from additional reading and then synthesizing our sources.

In fact, writers, like Andrew, often "discover" and pursue a new thesis idea, often much more narrowed, suggested by the gathered research. For example, Andrew may have assumed that community policing principles were already well known and ingrained in police agencies. However, in the course of interviewing practitioners Andrew realized that the original "recipe" for community policing had either never been widely understood/learned or had been so changed in the way it was practiced that its effectiveness had been greatly diminished. As a result, he realized that he would need to restate the "correct" basics of community policing in his paper and, at the same time, to show how it could be highly effective in addressing virtually any crime problem.

THESIS DEVELOPMENT FLOWCHART

While books encourage us to believe that writing is a linear process, it isn't. Instead, writing is a recursive process, meaning we keep going back to readjust what we have already done. Look at the flowchart below, focusing on the thesis statement that seems to capture this idea of moving forward and backward.

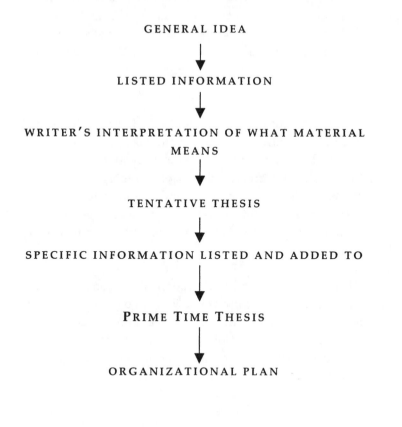

GENERAL IDEA

↓

LISTED INFORMATION

↓

WRITER'S INTERPRETATION OF WHAT MATERIAL MEANS

↓

TENTATIVE THESIS

↓

SPECIFIC INFORMATION LISTED AND ADDED TO

↓

PRIME TIME THESIS

↓

ORGANIZATIONAL PLAN

STEP FOUR: DRAFTING

Many students (not our readers, of course) define **drafting** as the process of sitting at the computer for many hours, preferably after midnight, to begin and finish a paper due for class the next morning. Then, in order to make sure the paper is perfect, they run a quick spell check before printing and dash for class, clutching their efforts that in daylight look considerably less brilliant than they did at 4:00 am. The bottom line is that haste does not produce quality. The express lane may be great for grocery store shopping but not for paper writing

As you may guess, the definition we will use for "**drafting**" will show significant differences from the process above. For us, **drafting** means the process when ideas are translated into words, sentences, paragraphs, and then revised to provide for clear communication to readers. And even more importantly, this process requires time to let writing "cool" before coming back to reconsider, rearrange, and revise.

Therefore, the hyper-speed paper method many students try unsuccessfully to use won't work, in part because of our brains. Thinking and translating ideas into words is a higher-level brain function and looking at relationships among words in order to state information clearly is also a higher-level brain function.

Quite simply, our brains cannot perform both tasks at one time, needing to choose between the thinking stage and the writing stage at any one time. Yet, both thinking and writing are important to produce an effective writing product. We need to think logically and then to state our ideas clearly, guided by assessment of readers' "entry behavior": what do they already know, what do they need to know in order to understand, and what is the best way to state information for them. (Sound familiar? See Chapter One.)

Our first step in the writing process is to focus on developing the paper's content by determining an organizational plan for writing.

DETERMINING AN ORGANIZATIONAL PLAN

When we choose a plan for organizing the entire paper, we make a selection based on how information will be best understood by readers. This differs from a content outline, reflecting the specific content of the paper. Instead the organizational plan is more an overview of how the paper will fit together. When we understand how the paper will be organized, we are then able to decide where specific information can be placed.

ORGANIZATIONAL PLAN CHOICES

There are general, overall organizational plans writers can use, but the choice to be considered in terms of the paper's **task, readers, scope**. In the academic world, the writer often selects an organizational plan unless a specific format to be followed is given. Keeping that in mind, let's look at the general descriptions of organizational plans.

General to Specific

This organizational plan is based on deductive reasoning where the writer begins with a general statement followed by more specific information (examples). Note that this pattern makes the main point immediately and then goes on to develop supporting details and assumes the reader will agree with the general statement.

A possible example here could be for a writer to state that efficient police call handling (general) can be traced to mobile digital terminals (specific).

Specific to General

This organizational plan is based on inductive reasoning where the writer starts with the specific and moves to the more general. Often this pattern is used to give the reader time to consider individual, specific pieces of information before the writer indicates what they add up to. This is especially useful when the reader may be unfamiliar with the paper's focus or may not initially be likely to agree with the general statement.

We unfortunately have recent examples of this pattern. Consider the attempts to determine who was responsible for mailing anthrax, killing several people (specific) with no one convicted of this crime (general).

CHRONOLOGICAL

This organizational plan uses time to determine the sequence of ideas. This is a common pattern for narration in fiction and history but often is not the most effective method for presenting more complex information requiring analysis.

This pattern could be used to list the legislative initiatives, focusing on a Criminal Justice issue in chronological order.

SPATIAL

This organizational plan uses physical location to determine the order information is given.

This organizational pattern could be used to develop an agency's reportage line or to describe a crime scene.

CAUSE/EFFECT

Just as it sounds, this pattern focuses on what has caused something to develop a pattern, trend, etc. and then discusses the effects produced as a result.

For example, a writer might want to develop the causes of an increase in gang activity in a certain location and then discuss the effects in certain identified areas, such as economic development, injury and death rate, deterioration of existing structures, etc.

ANDREW'S ORGANIZATIONAL PLAN

Let's look at Andrew's tentative organizational plan to answer the sample questions. To refresh your memory, let's look at the sample assignment again.

Sample Assignment

The field of law enforcement provides a wide variety of research opportunities, interesting to both students and practitioners. Therefore, the purpose of this paper is first to ask you to identify a research topic that provides recent information to law enforcement practitioners that would be helpful to them in their crime prevention mission. To help you select a current topic, please review current CJ publications and/or interview law enforcement practitioners to gather possible ideas.

Then, after you have selected a writing topic, prepare a research paper that summarizes at least three key aspects of the current CJ area relating to crime prevention you have chosen you judge practitioners would need to know in order to understand the information. The paper should be approximately ten pages, using at least five different research resources. All resources should be documented using APA documentation format. The due date is October 21, and the paper is worth 30 percent of the course grade.

As an added incentive to perform well on this exercise, a review panel of local police chiefs will read each paper to determine which three papers best address topics of urgent value to law enforcement.

Andrew's tentative organizational plan to answer the sample assignment's questions follows.

- Thesis statement, reflecting effectiveness of community-oriented policing in crime reduction in gangs, drugs, terrorism and police departments' misunderstanding of community oriented policing principles

- Definition of community-oriented policing (COP)
- Summary of police departments' misunderstanding of COP
- COP theory/practices that help prevent crime-develop each in detail
- SARA method
- Broken windows
- Normative sponsorship & critical social theory

Show how lack of complete understanding of COP principles/practices listed above greatly reduces effectiveness in crime reduction (Handle each practice and effect of misunderstanding separately or all principles/practices together? Try both ways to decide what works better.).

CRIMINAL JUSTICE ORGANIZATIONAL PLANS

In contrast to academic writing that less frequently specifies the pattern of organization, professional writing in Criminal Justice often uses predetermined organizational plans, especially in standard reports.

As a Criminal Justice professional, you will become very familiar with standard formats for reports. These formats, creating a writing plan that predetermines where specific information is located, makes it possible to identify where information is carried in the document and ensures that information is complete.

To illustrate, let's consider the organizational plans for some typical CJ reports.

Administrative Report	Investigative Report
(category)	(category)
RESEARCH REPORT	PRE-SENTENCE INVESTIGATION REPORT
Background	Offender's Personal Information
Analysis	Victim impact statement
	Criminal history
Recommendations	Recommendation
	Probation plan

DEVELOPING A WRITING PLAN

Once the writer determines the basic organizational plan for the writing project, the next step is to create a writing plan to determine how information will be structured in the paper. As writers follow the following steps, individual preferences emerge. Some writers, particularly those in the more technical fields, may find an outline essential to begin writing. Outline forms may range from a blueprint approach with each detail listed to a more general topic outline.

Other writers, who may not find an outline approach useful, begin with a general idea of what needs to be included but create a series of drafts in order to develop content and discover where material should be placed, using a cut-and-paste method to extract good material from all the drafts to arrive at a final draft.

Writers need to determine what works for them. In most cases there is not a significant difference in completion time, but the emphasis here is in finding a method that produces successful results for you. Interestingly, many writers still follow the rather arbitrary rules set forth by their seventh grade English teacher, never understanding that, within the writing process, many possible approaches exist.

Whatever process a writer chooses, the list below offers **general planning suggestions.**

1. Look again at reader analysis bullets (Chapter 1), remembering that your goal is to communicate effectively with the readers.
2. Make sure you have completed the gathering of information and necessary thinking before you begin to write.
3. Have all the reference material at hand so you can provide required documentation for information to avoid plagiarizing.
4. Identify the sections of the paper you will need to support the thesis statement and develop ideas completely
5. Budget your time to write **one** section at a time, taking a break before moving on to write the next section.
6. Build paper sections that logically flow from previous sections to the next section.

PLAGIARISM

As writers begin to draft, they incorporate researched materials into the body of the papers, which raises the issue of plagiarism.

It would be hard to determine whether plagiarism ranks higher than others on the academic dishonesty scale, but it certainly attracts our attention. At the professional writing level, we are aware of the plagiarism controversy involving respected historians Stephen Ambrose and Doris Kearns Godwin. Both, noted historians, apparently used minor sources, undocumented, in their publications. In each case, a source was very familiar to the writer, and plagiarism occurred when Ambrose and Kearns used exact wording of the original source, incorrectly thinking it was the writer's own thinking.

At the instructional level, we see web sites offering advice and software to detect plagiarism ("Just type in a sequence of five words...") competing with sites selling papers, offering advice on personalizing them to avoid detection.

So, what's the big deal about plagiarism? Quite simply, it's the attempt, deliberate or unintentional, to pass off someone else's work as your own. While some students do deliberately set out to be dishonest, most others do so by failing to acknowledge (**cite**) their sources or document sources correctly and, by default, plagiarize. Remember, if it's not your original thinking, you need to give credit (**citing**) to the original source. <u>No matter how you use the information--quotation, paraphrase, summary- material must be cited</u>.

Documentation does more for the reader than establish ownership. On a more practical level, documentation of sources provides a real service to readers. By providing references, the writer allows the reader to find easily the original material and read it in its entirety. In a sense, it's not too different from a web site link on our computer screen, alerting us to additional information.

STYLE MANUALS

Even though writers know that they must document sources, how then can they avoid unintentionally plagiarizing sources used in the paper? The best answer to that is buy a reference manual that discusses and gives examples of correct **documentation formats** for different types of sources, including books, periodicals, journals, on-line sources, interviews, Internet sites...

Before buying, the writer should determine which **style manual** is used in the discipline because formats will vary. For example, <u>Publication Manual of the American Psychological Association,</u> or APA, is frequently used in Criminal Justice writing while <u>The Modern Language Association,</u> or MLA manual, is used in the Humanities. Instructors often list the required documentation format in the course syllabus or can offer correct purchase information.

WRITING DECISIONS: QUOTATION, SUMMARY, PARAPHRASE

Now that we know how to find the correct way to document all different types of sources, we need to decide how best to present the information in the body of the paper. While quotations, summaries, and paraphrases carry our researched information and require documentation, they are used somewhat differently.

QUOTATIONS

Quotations make writers comfortable. After all, the writer needs only to write the exact words, place them inside quotation marks, and give the source. In fact, some writers feel so comfortable using quotations that their papers seem to be made up of a string of quotations with very little writing to connect them. It's almost as if the writer has cut and pasted original sources in the paper.

While there's nothing like a good quotation that gets to the heart of the matter and states things so well, nothing is more deadly than reading a series of quotations that seem to be there because the writer didn't know how to extract the necessary information from the rest of the quotation. Generally speaking, if the source provides narration, as our example below, a **quotation** is **not** a good choice for sharing information with readers.

Look at the following magazine paragraph about the recent arrest of Jose Padilla, accused of planning to detonate a "dirty bomb" in Washington, D.C.

> Padilla first surfaced in February when he went to the American Consulate in Karachi to get his new passport. The consulate, suspicious of a Hispanic with an assumed Muslim name in Pakistan, later flagged U. S. intelligence operatives, including FBI investigators. Not long afterward, American officials say, Pakistani authorities detained Padilla and a non-American associate for investigation on possible immigration violations, then let them go. (Hosenball, Hirsch, & Moreau, 2002, p. 32)

Notice the quote forces the reader to read more than is necessary rather than necessary. Writers who over quote rarely interpret the information; they just give it. This leaves the reader to try to extract the meaning the writer intended the reader should understand, woven into all those words. Expecting the reader to extract the necessary information is not a good writing strategy. First of all, there is a definite possibility readers will discover their own meaning that may not be the writer's interpretation. Secondly, reading quotations, especially those that shouldn't be quoted, can be deadly boring, encouraging readers to skim over content or stop reading altogether.

Are we trying to scare writers away from using quotations? No, but the point is that quotations are a bit like hot sauce: they get the reader's attention, often create a specific sensation, but, used too often or too much, the reader becomes irritated or immune to the effect.

Use a quotation when:
- the source is primary data(the actual document or piece of information that others write about)
- the quote is from a highly respected person or a recognized authority in the field
- the wording is so well stated or precise it could not be effectively restated
- the writer disagrees with the source and wants to establish fairly and precisely what was stated (Booth, Colomb, & Williams, 1999, p. 174)

Remember that, because we write for others, we must interpret or explain the quotation, always relating it to the points we make.

SUMMARY

Summaries operate in somewhat an opposite direction because they <u>sum</u> up the important points of the original article in an abbreviated form. Most often summaries are used to provide background information or explanation to readers when the writer determines it is not necessary for readers to read the original source but to have access to <u>all</u> the information.

There is no exact word count for summaries although some texts suggest approximately one-fourth of the length of the original. Regardless of length, if the summary is to serve as a substitute for the original, writers need to be concerned that it:

- states the source's thesis statement
- is a condensed version of the original
- is objective, eliminating writer's opinion
- is complete, reflecting all major points rather than certain aspects only

PARAPHRASES

A paraphrase is another strategy to avoid excessive quoting and exists between the summary and the quotation. Like the summary, the paraphrase is stated in the writer's words, and, like the quotation, the paraphrase states each idea contained in the original source in approximately the same number of words. Paraphrases can be powerful because they allow the reader to give the detail of the original ideas without being locked into the language of the quotation. Often paraphrases can state information in words that readers may find easier to understand.

Yet there can be problems. How do you rewrite the material in your own words without either:

- creating awkward, strange writing
- **shadow plagiarizing,** that is, creating sentences whose word choice and sentence structure are so close to the original as to almost be the original source's "evil twin"?

The following suggestions should offer direction to writing effective paraphrases.

The writer should:

1. rewrite material from the original source in approximately the same number of words.
2. give an in-text citation for the source, using the discipline's style manual
3. keep those words from the original source that are so well stated a better choice doesn't exist, but put quotation marks around them.
4. reflect the original tone of the source with verb choice, i.e., "complains," "praises," "explains" to place the paraphrase within the context of author's attitude toward the subject.
5. look at the original source only when finished to determine if the paraphrase reflects the meaning and avoided wording of the original (shadow plagiarizing)
6. use quotation marks around any words from the original source (Lester, 1999, p.112)

REFERENCES

Booth, W.C., Colomb, G.G., & Williams, J.M. (1999). *The craft of research.* Chicago: The University of Chicago Press.

Hosenball, M., Hirsch, M., & Moreau, R. (2002, June 24). *Odyssey into the shadows.* Newsweek, 139(25), 28-35.

Lester, J. (1999). *Writing research papers: a complete guide (9th ed.).* New York: Longman.

STEP FIVE:
REVISING AT THE CONTENT LEVEL

The previous chapters offered guidelines for writers to generate ideas, evaluate their writing possibilities, find and evaluate research sources, and develop an organizational plan for the paper that should result in a final draft that will need minor revisions rather than full-scale reconstruction.

Because our brains can't revise content and writing at the same time, a writer performs two different levels of revision. This chapter deals with content revision, always performed before the writer examines writing at the sentence, word and punctuation levels.

THE NEED FOR CONTENT REVISION

You may be wondering why, after following all the steps, <u>any</u> revision is necessary. Isn't it logical to expect you now have a paper that is ready to be turned in? In an ideal world, the answer would be "yes," but, in the real world, even the most carefully planned paper will have weaknesses that the writer needs to resolve before finalizing the paper. In other words, a discrepancy always exists between the content of the planned paper and the actual draft, not because the writer has done something wrong, but instead, because of continued thinking as the writer drafts.

Good reasons exist for writers' need to make content adjustments to the draft, adjustments that cannot be previously "planned away." However, adjustment decisions in general do not require the emergency thinking demanded of writers looking at the results of their papers where no planning or serious thinking had been done beforehand.

To illustrate the expected difference between the planned paper and the actual written draft, let's go back to examine Andrew's organization plan, developed in Chapter 4, to answer the sample question. Remember that the focus of the question was on three key CJ aspects relating to crime prevention. (The complete question appears in Chapters 1 and 4)

ANDREW'S ORGANIZATION PLAN

PLANNING SHEET

Here is a copy of Andrew's preliminary planning sheet for answering the sample question.

Thesis statement- effectiveness of community oriented policing in crime reduction and police departments' misunderstanding of community oriented policing principles
- Definition of community oriented policing (COP)
- Summary of police departments' misunderstanding of COP
- COP theory/practices that help prevent crime - gangs, drugs, terrorism*develop each SARA method
  Broken windows
  Normative sponsorship & critical social theory

Note: Police departments' lack of complete understanding of COP principles/practice makes it hard for them to have much impact on crime prevention.(Handle each practice and effect of misunderstanding separately or together???? Try both ways to see what works.)

WRITING PROJECT EVALUATION

Task-to discuss at least 3 key aspects of CJ area (SARA, broken windows, normative sponsorship) and crime prevention-gangs, drugs, terrorism
Scope-10 pages- should be enough to develop it.
Readers- Instructor primary reader but police officers as later readers. Discussion of features of COP to show instructor my mastery of material, and emphasis on how COP is misused by police departments will make it interesting and applicable to police officers.

ANDREW'S DRAFT PROBLEM

Based on this planning, can we predict smooth sailing for Andrew and predict he will have little or no revision? NO.

Let's look at the potential problems Andrew's plan has, something that he will probably not recognize until he examines his draft. The good news, though, is that, because of his careful thought and planning, he should be able to identify problems to resolve them.

While Andrew's outline shows logical thinking and good planning, he may not recognize that the paper has potential problems. Note that Andrew's plan develops two separate strands of thought:

- 3 aspects of COP that specifically relate to crime
- police officers' misunderstanding of COP

While the ideas are interrelated, each could be developed as a separate paper, one devoted to COP elements useful in crime prevention; the other focused more on police departments' misuse of COP because of lack of emphasis on the police public partnership.

In fact, if we look at the first paragraph of Andrew's draft, we can see the problem already emerging. Take a look.

> The purpose of this report is to identify and summarize key aspects of the <u>community-oriented policing (COP) philosophy</u>. This theme was identified after a literature review and interviews of local law enforcement personnel. The literature review revealed that COP is integral to crime prevention. Whether the issue is gangs, drugs, or terrorism, the research showed that COP, when properly applied, provided an effective means for dealing with crime. <u>One of the biggest impediments to universal acceptance of COP is that it is widely misunderstood</u>. <u>Few police agencies seem to practice it in its most effective manner.</u> For example, it is common to see limited application of its core feature: a police-public partnership.

In sentence 1, Andrew writes he will "identify and summarize key aspects of COP" and then in sentence 5 identifies COP as being less effective because its principles are misunderstood. Because each of these strands could be a separate paper, Andrew's opening paragraph seems to promise more than he can develop in a <u>ten-page</u> paper.

In addition to trying to develop COP and police officers' misunderstanding, Andrew also indicates that COP effectiveness in crime prevention will be discussed within the contexts of "gangs, drugs, or terrorism," the very areas we recognized needed to be narrowed in Chapters 1 and 2. Andrew could not discuss COP and all gangs, all drugs, and all terrorism in this paper, or perhaps in any paper. Broad topics like these are better suited to a series of long publications.

PREDICTING ANDREW'S DRAFT

Using Andrew's writing plan, we could predict writing sections of the draft would look something like the following.

Section 1-thesis statement

Section 2-discuss/define COP (This could take several paragraphs to several pages). At this point his writing plan indicates he will write about <u>COP in general</u>, and even if he devotes several pages to it, he will be writing about it at a general information level rather than developing specifics.

Section 3-discuss what police officers don't seem to understand/apply about COP. Here's where much of the difficulty begins. Before he has identified the three aspects of COP relating to crime prevention, Andrew's plan shows he will discuss what officers don't do to implement effectively the <u>very aspects Andrew has yet to discuss.</u> Therefore, the paper's logic is beginning to break down.

Section 4-discuss 3 aspects of COP that relate to crime reduction in gangs, drugs, terrorism. If your hair is beginning to stand on end when you look at this section, it should. Look at everything that would have to be covered: SARA, broken windows, normative sponsorship, each one's relationship in crime reduction, as applied to the very broad areas of gangs, drugs and terrorism.

To summarize, because Andrew probably will not recognize the preliminary problems he has created when he

developed his writing organization plan, his draft will try
to develop the link between COP and crime prevention,
police department misunderstanding and misuse of COP,
and its effectiveness against gangs, drugs, and terrorism,
leaving Andrew with a draft that will be able to hit only the
surface of each area, supported by general information
only.

POSSIBLE SOLUTIONS TO ANDREW'S DRAFT PROBLEMS

While he may feel panicked by the results, Andrew can still
develop a good paper from this shaky start if he diagnoses
the problem as the too broad focus, implied in the first
paragraph, and narrow it. He should consider:
1. the match between what is written and the
    assignment's writing task
2. which subject area best meets the assignment task
3. how to eliminate/narrow ideas within each area —
    "gangs," "drugs," "terrorism
4. a modified **thesis statement** that shows what will
    be supported in the paper (A possible thesis
    statement might be "Communities can effectively
    reduce gang-related crime through application of
    community-oriented policing principles whose
    effectiveness requires a strong relationship between
    the community and its police force.")

The point we are making is that the draft reflects our
thinking **at a particular point**. Later, when we see evidence
of our thinking in our draft, we have the opportunity to
reevaluate and revise as necessary. It's an expected part of
the writing process, one that, no matter how competent we
are as writers, can be skipped.

THE PLANNED PAPER VS. THE ACTUAL DRAFT

Andrew's draft problem involved rethinking the entire paper, and while serious, we saw it could be solved. Even a draft that has a strong thesis statement can have problems in content development.

TYPICAL DRAFT CONTENT PROBLEMS

The following list identifies typical draft content problems that the writer must solve before finalizing the paper. Some of the more common problems are:

1. Some sections of the paper seem weaker than others.
2. The required length is longer than what you have written.
3. Gaps in information exist, forcing the reader to guess about missing content.
4. The paper develops an idea originally not intended or is over weighted toward a particular idea.
5. The thesis no longer seems to reflect the developed content.

POSSIBLE SOLUTIONS FOR DRAFT PROBLEMS

WEAKER SECTIONS

It is natural to expect that some sections of the paper will be stronger than others, either because you had more gathered information to develop the section or found it easier to write that particular section. However, the writer needs to be concerned when a section is obviously underdeveloped compared to others or lacks specifics needed to develop/support it. That's when the writer needs to evaluate the cause of the section weakness.

One possible cause for a weak section is that it makes a very minor point, or even an unintended one without a strong connection to the paper's main content ideas and could be eliminated from the paper without eliminating necessary content. If the information from this underdeveloped section is reflected in the thesis statement, the thesis statement will need to be revised so that readers don't expect to find the information somewhere in the body of the paper.

On the other hand, the writer has a more serious problem if the problem with a weaker section stems from lack of necessary information to develop the section, or the writer doesn't understand how the information fits together and has been deliberately vague, hoping instead that the reader already knows the answers. In this case, the writer has no choice but to provide more information by conducting more research and understanding it. To eliminate points because it's easier for the writer will produce a seriously flawed paper.

LENGTH PROBLEMS

Writers in this situation often make the worst possible decision: they decide to pad the paper, repeating general information over and over, adding extraneous information, hoping to add required pages without adding valuable content. This padding seldom lends itself to brilliant observations, producing about the same result in the reader as being put on "hold" on the telephone, forced to listen to Muzak.

Therefore, the best first step to avoid attempts to try to make less look like more is for the writer to look at the assignment to make certain no part of it was left unanswered. If certain parts have not been addressed, the problem is fairly easy to resolve by answering the remaining questions.

On the other hand, if the writer evaluates all questions have been answered but the paper is still too short, other options exist. One possibility is for the writer to examine the paper, noting areas that seem underdeveloped or contain rather general content to make it more specific. Another tactic is to examine the examples and supporting information to determine whether adding additional support would strengthen (and lengthen) the paper.

If all points are developed and supported with adequate information, the writer needs to focus on the thesis statement, determining whether an additional, relevant idea should be added to it. In other words, the paper may be less than the required length because the thesis statement excludes some content areas needed to answer the question.

GAPS IN INFORMATION

The most obvious approach here is for writers to look at the gathered research to determine whether the material for whatever reason was not included. If, however, material needed to fill in the gaps doesn't exist, the writer will have to continue gathering information

PAPER TAKES ON DIFFERENT DIRECTION

Sometimes the draft turns out to be very different from what the writer thought/planned. In some cases it could be that a minor point in the original plan now becomes the draft's major focus. In other cases, the paper has drifted away from the intended thesis to develop something quite different.

In both cases, when the discrepancy exists, the writer needs to distinguish whether the draft is very off-focus or whether it is a better idea for the writer to develop in the paper. If the "new" content is merely getting off the subject, then the writer will probably need to eliminate it. However, if it seems like a better idea or a more focused idea than the original, the writer will want to revise the thesis statement to reflect this new, improved direction.

Thesis Statement Problems

(See discussion above.) Frequently, a writer has to adjust the thesis statement after reading the draft. This new thesis statement, which we labeled "Primetime Thesis Statement" in the flowchart at the end of Chapter 3, is a logical extension of the writer's evaluation of the draft. Very few writers can avoid making even minor changes to the thesis statement, necessary to reflect the revised, drafted content.

What Does Revision Say About Me?

Writers need to move beyond the point of ego, thinking that they, among all others, have mastered the art of perfect writing on the first try. Literary history is filled with stories of professional writers who struggled to produce what became masterpieces after many revisions or were forced to abandon the entire project because it couldn't be brought under control to meet readers' needs.

Content revision is a necessary part of writing. As we continue to change our perspective or reevaluate on the basis of additional information, we also need to readjust our drafts to reflect these content change. Often the draft, a written record of our thoughts, looks less clear than what we thought we had planned for, requiring us to add and delete, reorganize information, tasks our brain can't do perfectly in one draft.

REVISION AT THE PARAGRAPH LEVEL

Writing for readers carries the responsibility of conveying information in a pattern that they can easily follow and remain interested in what we are developing. While content development has been the major focus of this chapter, writers also want to look at paragraphs that should develop one idea, stated in the topic sentence.

FUSED PARAGRAPHS

As a reading cue, the topic sentence serves as a guide to the reader's eye about what information is contained within the paragraph, making it easy for the reader to find or refer back to information when re-reading the material. Therefore, all information in the paragraph should relate to the topic sentence; any other information should be eliminated or moved to another paragraph to avoid reader confusion.

The common writing term used to describe paragraphs that develop more than one idea is "fused paragraphs." If your instructor has ever written on your paper, 'Too many ideas in this paragraph," you weren't being complimented on your ability to think. Instead, you had fused paragraphs. Look at the example below where the underlined sentence shows how a new idea has been fused to the paragraph.

Technology has also improved the way our hospitals function and our health. Doctors now are able to perform surgery without needing to make an incision, speeding up patient recovery time. Medical testing has also become more accurate, able to diagnose problems often before the patient has symptoms, and computers now store patient records that can be accessed rapidly by many different medical personnel. Some major hospitals have telecommunication links with other hospitals to provide additional information about patients seen at other hospitals. How people entertain themselves has also changed because of technology....

Obviously, the underlined sentence shows a shift in direction and the problem resolved by shifting the sentence into its own new paragraph and then adding supporting details. But, since it was so easy spot the shift in thought, is it really necessary to "de-fuse" paragraphs? YES. Keep in mind that readers have not had the opportunity to follow you through the idea generating stage, the search for research, the organizational planning. The first time they know what you are thinking about is when they read your final draft.

If paragraphs are the basic building block of the paper, then you have to be careful that they don't contain different strands of thought, seldom developed, having a vague connection to other material that only the writer understands. This, in turn, confuses the reader and dulls the original point of the paragraph. Why is that your problem? For three reasons:

- you are writing to communicate to the reader
- reading comprehension drops dramatically when a reader is confused and has to reread.
- bored readers often become non-readers (except for your instructor who is a captive reader, but then, most of your professional writing will not be done for an instructor.)

PARAGRAPHS WITHOUT SUPPORTING INFORMATION

Paragraphs that lack enough supporting detail should be the ones writers identify when they identify gaps in information in their writing. These problem paragraphs seem to hint at so much without giving adequate supporting detail, almost challenging the reader to fill in the missing blanks. Sometimes the information is omitted because the writer fails to anticipate readers' needs or skips over the details either because the writer doesn't understand the connections or lacks the necessary research to supply details. Look at the lack of detail in the following paragraph.

> The rate of homicides committed by youths, aged 14-19, rose dramatically in the central part of the state. According to Police Chief Russell Smith, the largest increase was in vehicular homicide, now accounting for 10 per cent of all homicides in Brookview County. Chief Smith believes that the County should join

forces with MADD to resume their previous programming for teenagers to see if something could be done to reduce the alarming vehicular homicide rate.

CONTENT CHECKLIST FOR CAREFUL WRITERS

College juniors, enrolling at Pennsylvania State University at Harrisburg, took the Individual Writing Profile (IWP), a writing assessment tool designed to determine whether incoming students had the necessary writing skills to complete senior-college level assignments. All IWP writing samples were read and evaluated by two college instructors form outside the university and evaluated, using a Penn State-specific rubric, adapted from *Pennsylvania Writing Holistic Scoring Guide.* (Schmidt & Brode, 1994). The rubric sets up specific writing standards in seven different writing areas. The content standards listed below could serve as a quick checklist for writers to use when evaluating draft content.

CONTENT STANDARDS
FOCUS
- sustains a single point of view
- Answers the question

CONTENT
- Ideas are analyzed rather than named/listed
- Information and details are specific and relevant to the paper
- Paper develops a clear thesis and effective conclusion

ORGANIZATION
- Main points follow logical order or recognizable sequence
- Each paragraph deals with only one subject
- All paragraphs relate to the topic
- Logical transitions exist between sentences and between paragraphs

REFERENCES

Schmidt, J. H., & Brode, K.L. (1994). *Individual Writing Profile: Evaluative Criteria.*

Unpublished manuscript, Pennsylvania State University at Harrisburg.

STEP SIX:
REVISING AT THE SENTENCE LEVEL

The previous five chapters have focused on developing the content of a paper so that it moves along logically with appropriate supporting information. In this chapter, however, we turn the focus to the sentence level to determine if our ideas are expressed clearly to avoid reader confusion about content and prevent misreading.

Sometimes after struggling to refine the thinking of their papers, writers are distressed that their drafted sentences look so—well, awkward or juvenile. They think, "The content is complex, so why do my sentences look so poorly written?" These writers have forgotten what we said earlier about the brain not being able to think and craft sentences at the same time. Consequently, we can expect the paper's thinking may be clear and precise, but the actual wording of those ideas in sentences will always need some revision.

REVISION ELEMENTS AT THE SENTENCE LEVEL

If you are mentally groaning, thinking this chapter is about to launch into the usual review of sentence mechanics and punctuation, you will be disappointed that is not our direction. Instead, we're going to focus on revision techniques that help streamline writing to make sentences smoother, more precise, and less wordy <u>after</u> we remind you about the importance of sentence structure and punctuation.

THE TWO MINUTE MECHANICS REVIEW

That we are not going to discuss mechanics and punctuation in no way indicates we think they are unimportant. But we know that so many other sources, probably including the textbook you used for Introduction to Composition, do such a thorough job in offering writing mechanics explanations and examples that we could not do the subject justice in so few pages. In case you no longer own that writing manual, many colleges have web sites, usually linked to learning centers, offering similar information for your reference. For example, Purdue University's web site (<u>www.purdue.edu</u>) has excellent resources for writers.

Because we would be negligent in not even mentioning standard correction areas to evaluate writing at the sentence level, the following chart lists them for you.

Correction Areas
Sentence Structure Complete sentences, avoiding fragments and run-ons Parallel construction Variety of sentence structures and sentence length
Writing Conventions Correct capitalization, punctuation and spelling Correct usage of pronouns, subject-verb agreement Avoidance of commonly mistaken words

ENSURING READABILITY THROUGH REVISION

While writers want to make certain that sentences are grammatically correct, they are aware that other revisions may be needed to ensure **readability.** This term means the reader's ability to read through a document without having to stop to reread confusing sentences or provide apparent missing links in the development of ideas.

You might be inclined to think it's really not that much of a problem. After all, the writer did all the work so can't the readers contribute something or use their imaginations? It's not quite that simple. If readers have to try to figure out what is being communicated, several outcomes can occur:

1. The readers' interpretations of the material may differ from the writer's intended meaning.
2. The readers' levels of reading comprehension decline after their eyes stop moving forward, having to go back to reread.
3. The readers may lose interest and stop reading altogether.

To ensure readability, we're going to look at four areas of revision: providing transitions, varying sentence pattern and length, choosing audience-appropriate language, and eliminating unnecessary words.

PROVIDING TRANSITIONS

Transitions, as you know, provide clues to the reader about the relationships between words and between sentences. By including well-chosen transitional words and phrases, the meaning is made clear, avoiding reader confusion or time to puzzle out the connections.

Categories of transitions exist, conveying different relationships. If your repertoire of transitions only includes, "in addition," "later," and "on the other hand," you will want to consult complete lists for those that convey very specific relationships among material including those that

- link similar ideas or add an idea
- limit or contradict an idea or show contrast
- indicate cause, reason, or result
- indicate time or spatial relationship
- indicate a following example
- indicate a comparison

Notice that the underlined transitions in the following sentences clarify sentence relationships.

John left his car running when he went into the store to pick up his dry cleaning. <u>Consequently,</u> the teenager who had just shoplifted several items from the convenience store jumped into John's car and sped out of the parking lot.

Officer Martin Carr is the new police chief in Chatham. <u>Previously,</u> he had been the deputy chief in Clearstream.

VARYING SENTENCE VARIETY AND LENGTH

When we write, we choose from 4 basic <u>sentence patterns</u>, each pattern ideally best suited to carry certain kinds of information. Understanding this correlation helps writers create less awkward sentences and increase reading comprehension.

Listed below are sentence patterns and the kind of information appropriate to each one.

1. Simple sentence-carries little information

The first study showed inconclusive results.

2. Compound sentence-carries two independent clauses whose information is equal in importance

Police recruits are trained in defensive techniques, and they learn COP techniques to relate to the community in a non-confrontational manner

3. Complex sentence-carries one idea clearly subordinate to the other

Because the car wouldn't start, John missed the 7:00 am train.

4. Compound-Complex sentence-carries equal and subordinate ideas

After Professor Smith finished seven years' of research for his book, it was published, and the College immediately promoted him to department chairman.

Writers also need to consider sentence length as a factor to ensure readability. If you are interested in pursuing this concept, you can find formulas that show you how to calculate readability rating of sentences, paragraphs, or entire papers. For our purposes, we will follow a general business guideline, indicating the average reader can comprehend meanings in sentences averaging 15 words per sentence. For us, as sentence writers, we will have some sentences with word counts shorter than 15 words and others of more than 15 words.

Why not make all sentences 15 words if that is the best length? Several answers to this question exist. First, while you may not consciously be aware of it, your brain registers repetition in language patterns so that the reader becomes bored with the repetition. We could compare this impression to hearing the same song played endlessly or eating the same food items at each meal. We become dulled by the experience.

Secondly, writers must consider the information the sentence will carry as a determining factor in optimal sentence length. If we are conveying more complex information, using less familiar terms or words of several syllables, the information must be carried in shorter sentences to allow the reader to process the message. When we need to convey dense content, we are wise to break the information into a larger number of sentences rather than one longer sentence because of reading comprehension.

If you doubt what we are saying, consider the last time you needed technical advice to troubleshoot a computer problem and called the help desk. After the attendant used "jewel case," "install drivers," and "IPO address" in the first sentence, you knew you couldn't put all the information together.

CHOOSING AUDIENCE-APPROPRIATE LANGUAGE

We have already discussed the importance of knowing who our readers will be, allowing us to determine which information will be used, where it will be placed, and, finally, how best to phrase material.

Often our research takes us to information written by authorities in the field, i.e. a medical researcher writing about advances in treatment for non-Hodgkin's lymphoma; an economist writing about Vroom's theory of motivation, a forensic scientist discussing new ways to evaluate trace elements of DNA. In those articles we often have to struggle to define for ourselves the more technical terminology, using dictionaries and cross-referencing from other sources to understand the content.

Our readers are often in a similar position of not understanding what we communicate to them. We can help by providing a means for understanding by offering a definition of terms and ideas, comparing the idea to something already familiar to our readers, or stating it in different terms. For example, our medical researcher above might refer to "adrenalechtomized mice" for a medical audience while non-medical readers would better understand the term as "mice that had adrenal glands removed." Note that both terms carry the same meaning, but each conveys it in audience- appropriate language.

While this seems an obvious example, be aware that all disciplines have their own terms and often create "new" words, often not in the dictionary, generally used only within the academic discipline or profession. We call such specific words or abbreviations **jargon**, and, as writers, we have to be aware that jargon does not carry the same meaning to readers outside the discipline/profession. For example, we might read about "M.O. detection" and "PSIR," terms that in all probability carry little meaning to those outside Criminal Justice fields. Therefore, it becomes even more important that we have identified all readers of our paper to determine when, and if, jargon conveys meaning to our readers.

ELIMINATING UNNECESSARY WORDS

Ironically, many people mistakenly believe strong academic and professional writing should not be understood by the average reader. They think the overly formal style of complicated sentences and elevated, often artificial, word choice, a sort of "showing off what you know," is necessary to reflect the importance of the content. Of course, the reader then needs to be willing to decode the message into easily understood information.

Fortunately, the newer emphasis on academic and professional writing is to make it accessible to its readers clearly and directly with a cleaner style, each word necessary for meaning. When writers use more words than necessary to convey information clearly and completely, they risk burying the meaning inside an avalanche of words, completely nullifying the original purpose for writing.

Perhaps writers should imagine they are charged twenty-five cents for each word used in the paper. The question they should ask about each sentences is "Did I get my money's worth?" If you look at information developed in the following sections to eliminate unnecessary word use, you should be able to say "Yes!"

REDUNDANCY

Redundancy is word choice that repeats the same idea. Probably all of us have heard the phrase "revert back," redundant because revert means "to go back," or heard advertisers warn us to order now to qualify for a "free gift," again ignoring the meaning of something given to, not paid for.

For your edification or amusement, can you identify why each of the following is redundant?

        close proximity
        biography of Ted Williams' life
        12 noon
        12 midnight
        shorter in length
        summarize briefly

We can also have redundancies within sentences where we repeat the same idea.

Pennsylvania moved to allow voter registration to drivers when they renewed their licenses. This was designed to encourage <u>unregistered voters who had not voted</u> to become involved in the election process. (Unless voter fraud exists, can't we assume this to be the case?)

PASSIVE VOICE

Verbs have two voices: active and passive. In active voice, the subject performs the action while in passive voice the subject is acted upon. Passive voice will always increase the number of words used.

The police officer <u>drove</u> the car. (active voice) 6 words
The car <u>was driven</u> by the police officer. (passive voice) 8 words

Notice that we have increased the number of words, changed the sentence subject from "police officer" to "car," and diminished the power of the verb to "was driven." Additionally, consistent use of passive voice is a guaranteed cure for insomnia because of the longer, dull sentences it produces. Readers have to be very curious to read through papers where the writer frequently uses passive voice. We offer the following paragraph as evidence.

The motion to approve the requirement that front doors be painted red by the occupants was passed. (passive) This bill had been sponsored by Martha Gladstone, owner of Ye Olde Paint Shoppe, and County Historian.(active) It was proposed last year but was defeated by a 7-3 vote against the provision.(passive)

Not only is the paragraph less interesting, it also leaves out crucial information: who performed the actions. Who approved the motion? Who defeated the proposal last year?

Contrast it with this example in active voice."The Commission on the Professionalization of Corrections Officers (CPCO) decided to continue discussion of increasing...." Here we know precisely who did what because active voice provides that information.

In short, passive voice increases word count and generally dulls sentence meaning. However, there are specific instances when writers consciously choose it.

1. when the actor is unknown or unimportant
   A 911call, reporting a possible homicide, was received at 12:42 am.
2. when identifying the actor would assess blame or liability
   A mistake was made in incorrectly flagging your account as overdrawn.

Combining Sentences

At the draft stage, sentences exist that don't carry enough information to warrant "spending" the words in weaker sentences. To eliminate this problem, sentences can be combined to make a stronger sentence or the content can be embedded within another sentence.

Embarrassingly, we have all written sentences like the following, short and choppy with a "Dragnet" feel to them. John went to the registrar's office. He couldn't schedule classes. There was a problem with his financial aid. (18 words) Notice the sentences are short and connected only because the <u>reader</u> carries over the information to the next sentence.

But, by combining sentences, we slightly reduce word count and more clearly show the relationship among sentence ideas.

John went to the registrar's office, discovering he couldn't schedule classes because of financial aid problems. (16 words)

In other cases, such as the example below, the writer may first need to look at sentence groups to analyze the sentence relationships before writing. The following sentences still have that disconnected feeling and we get duplication of ideas, "confused" and "didn't make sense" as well as word repetition.

The anthropologist was confused when he looked at the mummy. The death mask on the mummified remains of a laborer didn't make sense. Jeweled death masks were for pharaoh use only. (31 words)

Combined, a possible revision could combine three sentences into one sentence that is fairly long.

When the anthropologist looked at the jeweled death mask, used only for pharaohs, on the mummified remains of a laborer, he was confused. (23 words)

It could also be combined into two sentences, clearly reflecting the relationship.

When the anthropologist looked at the jeweled death mask on the mummified remains of a laborer, he was confused. These masks were used only for pharaohs. (26 words)

END NOTE

In some ways, *Effective Writing in Criminal Justice* seems equivalent to touring Europe in seven days: we have hit the major points of interest and, along the way, have pointed out where you can find more information on specific areas in writing.

Our goal in writing this manual was to develop a process for writing that is logical and efficient. Yet good writing requires practice and a willingness to keep experimenting before achieving successful results, so just reading it will not make you a better writer.

We hope, too, you realize that all writers continue to struggle with the results we produce, constantly rethinking, rewriting, and revising what is on our computer screen or tablet, in order to make our content meaningful to our readers.

APPENDIX A
PRACTITIONER RESEARCH REPORT
EXAMPLE

State of (Blank)
Department of Justice

MEMORANDUM
Date: May 31, 2002

To:	Long Range Planning Committee
	Kate O'Toole, Executive Director
From:	**Commission on Professionalization of**
	Corrections Officers
Subject:	**INCREASING THE CPT HOURLY**
	REQUIREMENT

Background
At its November 8, 2001, meeting the Commission on the
Professionalization of Corrections Officers (CPCO) decided
to continue discussion of increasing the Continuing
Professional Training (CPT) hourly requirement for
corrections officers to the July 2002 Commission meeting.
The concerns that were raised centered on perceived
budgetary and deployment shortfalls. The concerns are
summarized in *Attachment A.*

Analysis/Additional Research

Since the November Commission meeting, CPCO has conducted extensive research pursuant to the concerns cited. A stratified random sampling of small-, mid-, and large-sized agencies= CPT hours (*Attachment B*) was performed, as was an analysis of all correctional facilities statewide. The results of the descriptive analysis for calendar years 2000 and 2001 are shown in *Attachment C*.

In addition to the statistical computations, interviews were conducted with training managers and executives from small-, mid-, and large-sized correctional agencies. These interviews, which are summarized in *Attachment D*, illuminated numerous methods for accomplishing agencies= CPT objectives.

Benchmarking was conducted with other "Blank" public safety entities and select other professions to ascertain law enforcement=s standing among other professions= CPT standards. This analysis disclosed that among criminal justice and public safety practitioners, corrections personnel had the lowest standard for CPT. *Attachment E* contains the CPT mandates for all the entities comprising the comparison pool.

Conclusions

Research has disclosed that an increase in the number of CPT hours should not prove unduly burdensome for agencies, particularly when the value of increased training is weighed against the liability that can result from a failure to provide ongoing training in an amount commensurate with that provided other public safety personnel. The ability to meet expanded CPT hourly requirements is as much a function of quality management as any other single factor. Budgetary constraints will undoubtedly continue unabated in many quarters, but research has shown that inventive management can operate to offset virtually all but the most severe situations.

Recommendations
Staff recommends the Long Range Planning Committee consider the following alternatives:

1. Go forward with the originally recommended 40-hour biennial initiative, which represents an increase of eight hours per year, or

2. Consider a 32-hour biennial requirement, which represents an increase of four hours per year.

Note: The Committee may wish to consider as part of either alternative A1" or A2" an effective date for implementation, e.g., July 2005, that would enable correctional facilities to plan and budget incrementally for the increase in training.

APPENDIX B
ADMINISTRATIVE REPORTS

Administrative reports are generally non-criminal in content. They address matters of agency operations and can be either directed to an internal readership or to other government agencies or the public. These written communications generally fall into three categories: research, policies/procedures, and correspondence.

Research reports are not altogether unlike what you have been preparing in your college classes in the way of term papers. They address problems of concern to the agency or its stakeholders. Their structure is usually the same across criminal justice system components (i.e., police, courts, and corrections). At the outset a problem or concern is expressed. This leads directly into a description of the background of the subject of the report, i.e, a brief evolution of the situation. For example, recurrent questionable instances of use of force by police may prompt inquiry. Next, an in-depth analysis of the factors comprising the problem is conducted. With the use of force example, there may be examination of the agency's use of force policy, a look at other agencies' policies to see how similar situations are handled, review of training, and interviewing of citizens at large and recent detainees or arrestees. This is the most detailed and extensive portion of the report. It can also include tentative solutions, and the ramifications. The concluding portion of the report is a brief listing of recommendations, which is the product of the preceding analysis. With the use of force scenario, the recommendation can range from educating the public on the department's use of force policy to dismantling the existing policy.

Policies and procedures constitute the rules with which agencies must conform in performance of their missions. In some instances, these directives are legislatively mandated, e.g., sexual harassment or racial profiling. Procedures and policies are generally terse in their articulation, but they are the product of extensive interviewing and research. While these directives may be expressed in a few paragraphs, the stack of research paperwork that led to their creation may measure several inches in thickness. Almost all policies/procedures undergo legal review before they are promulgated, and in some instances they are subjected to public hearings before they can be incorporated into an agency's operational manual. Preparation of a directive is not as daunting a task as it may sound. Careful and thorough interviewing and research will get the job done properly.

Generally, policies and procedures are needed whenever there is a need to control, direct, or inform and for any issue that is important or benefits from clarification. Policies are broad guidelines that regulate organizational action. A policy is actually a type of position statement. It explains the organization's stand on a subject and why there is a rule about it.

If policies are the organization's guidelines, procedures are its "how to" statements. Procedures supplement the policy guidelines with specifics and complete the information users need. It is not sufficient to say, "it is our policy to provide the best client service anywhere" and stop there. Users need to know what that means. Procedures are action oriented. They outline the steps expected to be taken and the sequence in which the steps are to be performed (Campbell, 1998, pp. 1-6).

Correspondence is generally divided into two types: external and internal. External correspondence closely resembles the letters that we routinely prepare for sending to friends, relatives, or businesses. They contain the customary full address and salutation format. These are always on agency letterhead stationery. More often than not, external correspondence bears the signature block of the agency chief executive or other upper- echelon person. These letters may pertain to all matter of issues. Frequently, they are used to respond to citizen inquiries or complaints. External correspondence is also often used for agency-to-agency communications.

Internal correspondence uses custom forms and formats. There may be separate forms for office supplies requisition, for budgetary items, for use of travel funds, and myriad other special purposes. However, often there is a general correspondence format for routine communiques that do not already have a custom form. The general correspondence usually contains the following headings at the top of its first page: date, to, from, and subject. From this point on, depending on the message to be carried, the correspondence may be in flowing narrative form (almost like an external correspondence) or it may contain subheadings, e.g., background, analysis, and recommendations.

APPENDIX C
INVESTIGATIVE REPORTS

An investigative report is a written document that records in detail observations and actions as they relate to a specific incident or person. Each investigative report becomes a legal document that is a permanent record of information about an incident or individual. The criminal justice system cannot function without investigative reports, which are the documentation of facts prepared by the persons who have direct knowledge about a criminal situation. Three categories of reports are predominant: crime, arrest, and presentence investigation.

Crime Reports are used to provide written records of crimes reported to police. These type reports detail the preliminary investigation of a crime. They are generally succinct and record the elements of the crime being investigated, whether or not a criminal suspect has been apprehended. A crime report is the source document for the eventual filing of a criminal complaint with the prosecuting authority, which is really the initiation of full operation of the criminal justice process. These documents are reviewed with a good deal of scrutiny, especially by the defense counsel. Omissions of crucial information may constitute grounds for dismissal of the criminal case. Therefore, above all else it is vital crime reports are completed accurately and clearly. Every incident is different and different crimes require different information. However, all criminal investigation reports should contain: identification of the crime, identification of involved parties and their statements, crime scene specifics, property information (items stolen), and officers' actions (POST, 1999, p. 3-10).

The quality of report content is dependent on the reporting officer's ability to obtain information and statements from victims, witnesses, and suspects. Thus interviewing becomes very important. The key actions in this regard are attentive listening, note taking, and verification of information. Report formats may vary. Some jurisdictions require that certain information be noted on a standardized form, which is often used as the crime report cover sheet. When standardized forms are used it is important that all applicable check boxes are completed as this information may be input into an automated system for M.O. detection or crime pattern detections.

Arrest Reports are more detailed than crime reports because they must detail the all-important facts linking a specific suspected criminal offender with a particular crime. Complex issues such as "probable cause" (to search or to arrest) must be precisely articulated. Too, issues such as use of force or conditions under which statements are made by the suspect must be documented within the context they occurred. All of the guidelines cited for crime report completion certainly are pertinent to arrest reports.

Arrest reports involve more detailing than crime reports. Customary topics to be addressed in narrative form are the following: source of activity, officers' observations, arrest, booking, medical treatment, and use of force.

Presentence Investigation Reports (PSIRs) are prepared by probation officers to assist judges in their decision making. The PSIR is designed to advise a judge of the offender's criminal behavior, the options available for disposition, and the risks to society for whichever option the judicial authority may choose. The person who completes the PSIR carries a heavy responsibility since, given the work load under which courts labor, the recommendations contained in the PSIR are very often followed. Common subject areas covered in the PSIRs are as follows: offender's personal information, victim impact statement, criminal history, recommendation, and probation plan (Brown & Cox, 1998).

APPENDIX REFERENCE LIST

Brown, J.G., & Cox, C.R. (1998). *Report Writing for Criminal Justice Professionals*. Cincinnati, OH: Anderson.

California Commission on Peace Officer Standards and Training (1999). *Investigative Report Writing*. Sacramento, CA: Author.

Campbell, N. (1998). *Writing Effective Policies and Procedures*. New York: American Management Association.